Fierce Fighters

# NINJA

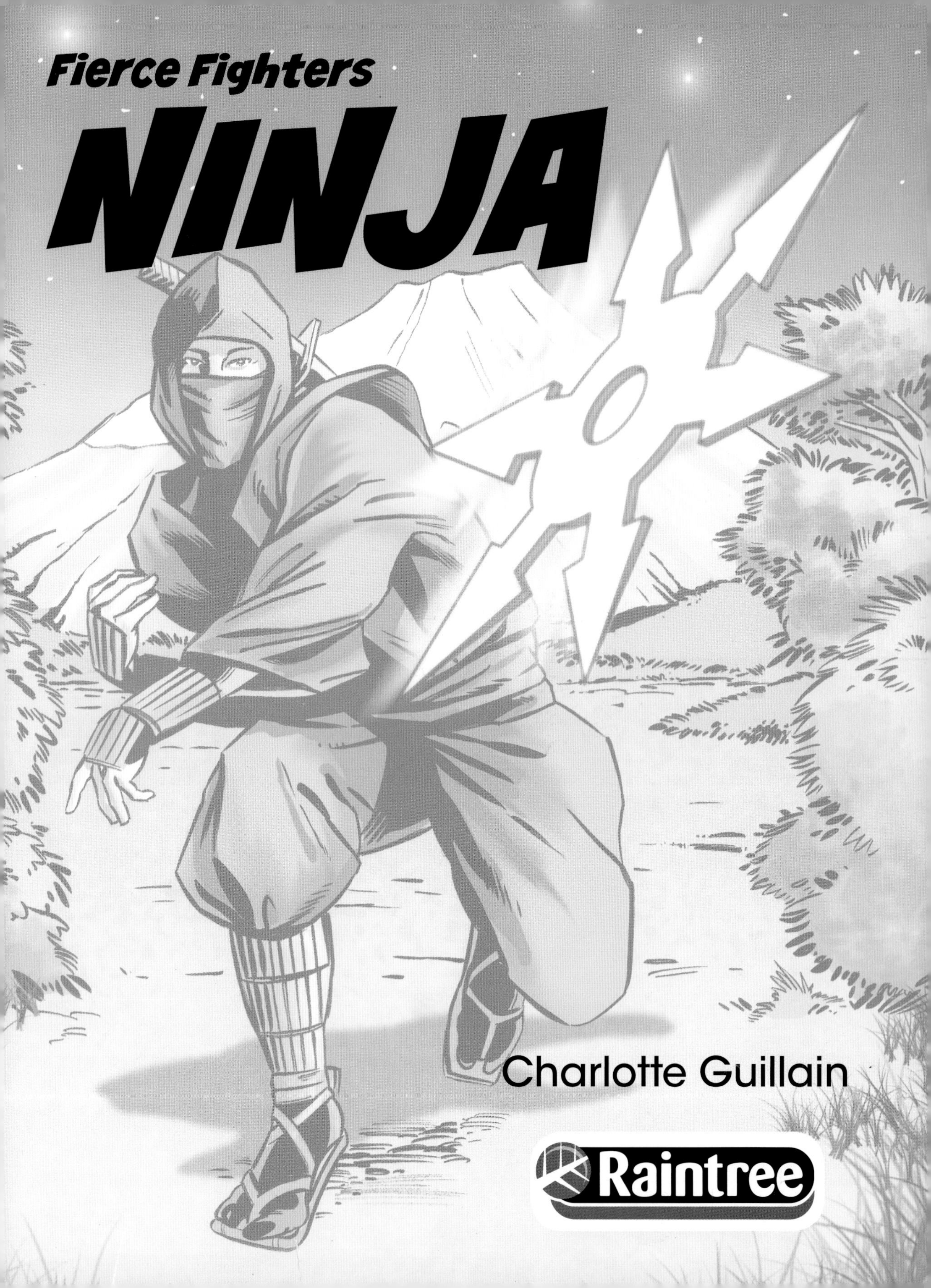

Charlotte Guillain

Raintree

**www.raintreepublishers.co.uk**
Visit our website to find out
more information about
Raintree books.

**To order:**
☎ Phone 0845 6044371
▤ Fax +44 (0) 1865 312263
▧ Email myorders@raintreepublishers.co.uk

Customers from outside the UK please telephone +44 1865 312262

Raintree is an imprint of Capstone Global Library Limited,
a company incorporated in England and Wales having its
registered office at 7 Pilgrim Street, London, EC4V 6LB
– Registered company number: 6695582

Text © Capstone Global Library Limited 2010
First published in hardback in 2010
The moral rights of the proprietor have been asserted.

Edited by Rebecca Rissman, Nancy Dickmann, and
Catherine Veitch
Designed by Joanna Hinton-Malivoire
Picture research by Tracy Cummins
Original illlustrations © Capstone Global Library 2010
Original illustrations by Miracle Studios
Production by Victoria Fitzgerald
Originated by Capstone Global Library
Printed and bound in China by Leo Paper Products

ISBN 978 1 406 21613 4
14 13 12 11 10
10 9 8 7 6 5 4 3 2 1

**British Library Cataloguing in Publication Data**
Guillain, Charlotte.
Ninja. -- (Fierce fighters)
355.1'0952-dc22

**Acknowledgements**
We would like to thank the following for permission to
reproduce photographs: Alamy pp. **21** (© Photo Japan),
**27** (© Photos 12); Getty Images pp. **8** (Emmanuel
Faure), **19** (Siegfried Layda), **23** (Chase Jarvis); Heinmann
Raintree pp. **28** (Karon Dubke), **29 top** (Karon Dubke),
**29 bottom** (Karon Dubke); Library of Congress Prints
and Photographs Division pp. **7**, **14**; Photolibrary
p. **9** (Charlie Schuck), **10** (PNC PNC); Shutterstock
pp. **13** (© Cristina CIOCHINA), **15** (© Martin Mette),
**17** (© Radu Razvan), **20** (© 3dfoto); THE KOBAL
COLLECTION p. **26** (WB/WEINSTEIN/IMAGI/MIRAGE);
The Granger Collection p. **16**.

Front cover illustration of a ninja warrior throwing a star
reproduced with permission of Miracle Studios.

The publishers would like to thank Jane Penrose for her
assistance in the preparation of this book.

Some words are shown in bold, **like this**. You can find
out what they mean by looking in the glossary.

# Contents

# Secret attack

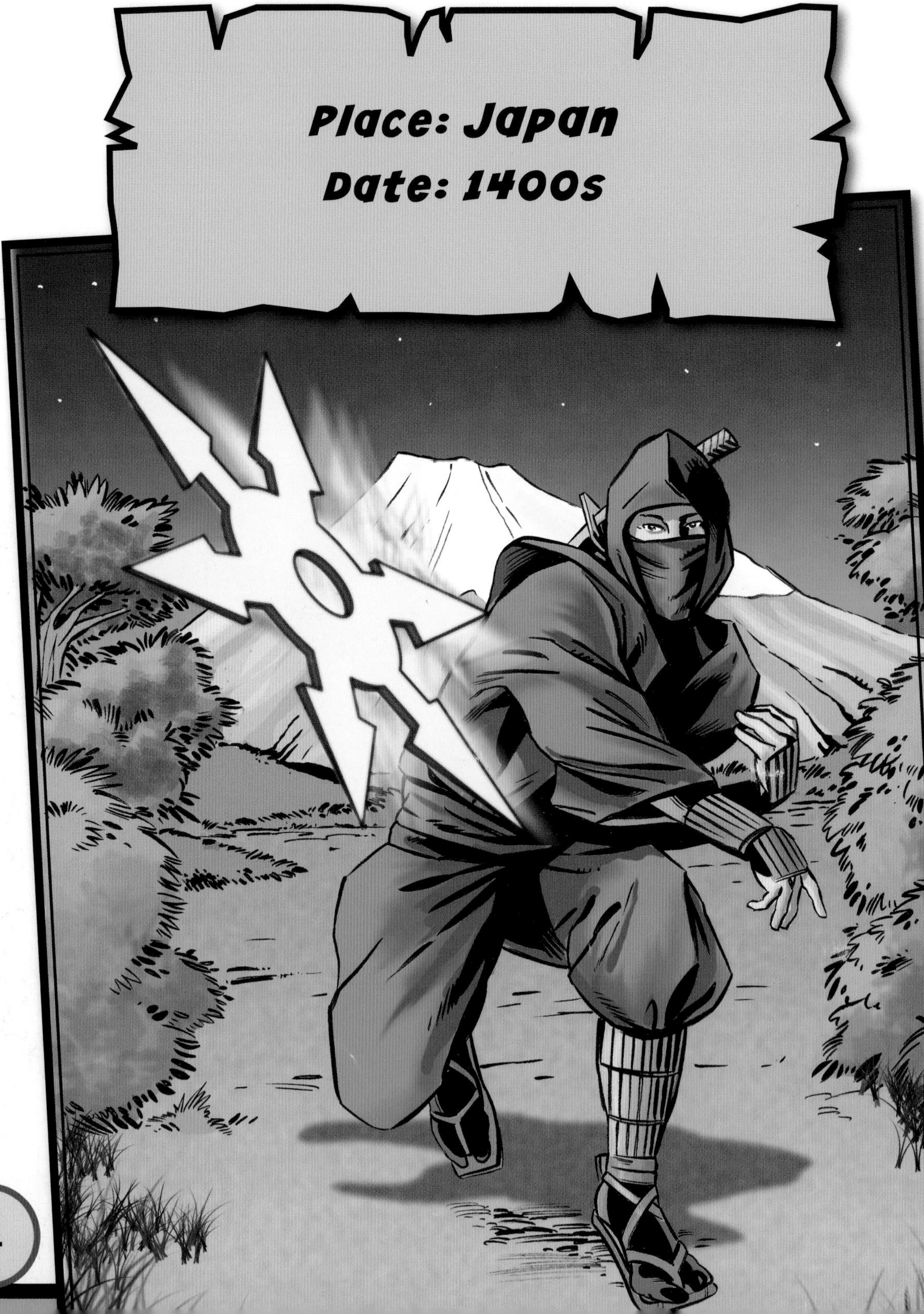

A dark figure slips through the shadows. He finds his enemy and pulls out a star-shaped blade. He throws his weapon and his enemy is dead.

Is anyone safe from a ninja attack?

## Ninja timeline

| | |
|---|---|
| **1400s** | Many rulers in Japan use ninja to fight enemies |
| **1550s** | Ninja starts to lose power |
| **1600s** | People from Europe start to settle in North America |
| **2000s** | You are reading this book |

# Who were the ninja?

The ninja were trained killers, called **assassins**. Assassins went on special **missions** to kill or injure enemies. Ninja fought in Japan from the 1400s to the 1600s.

## Where the ninja lived

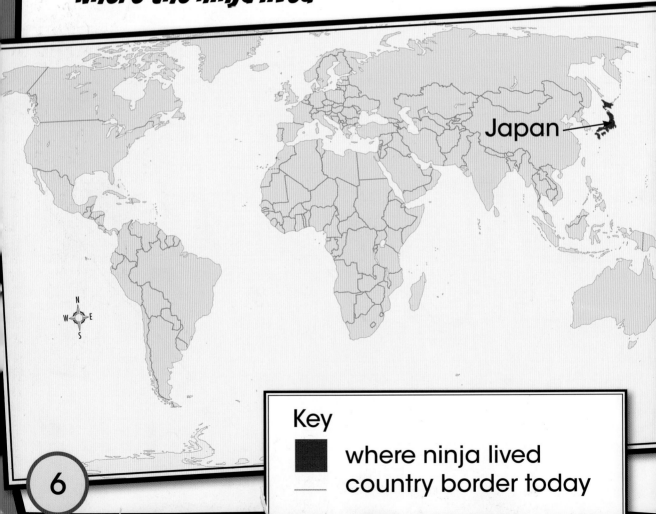

Japan

Key

■ where ninja lived

--- country border today

## DID YOU KNOW?

Only people in special families could be ninja.

# Becoming a ninja

Ninja families told their children the secrets of how to fight. Ninja children had to learn to be very tough. Children started training as soon as they could walk and talk. They learned to balance, jump, and hide.

You need to be able to balance well to do a ninja kick.

Older children learned to fight and **defend** themselves. Teenagers learned to use and hide special ninja weapons. They had to be tough, fit, and silent.

# Female ninja

Women could be ninja too. Women ninja were called *kunoichi* (say *koo-no-ee-chee*). Women ninja could use their beauty to get close to a **victim**. Then it was easy to kill him.

## DID YOU KNOW?

*Kunoichi* often pretended to be servants or dancers in an enemy's home to get close to him.

# Ninja missions

Ninja were like spies. Rulers used ninja to get information about their enemies or to kill them. Ninja could work quickly and silently. Often it was hard for people to know what had happened.

Rulers like this would have hired ninja to spy for them.

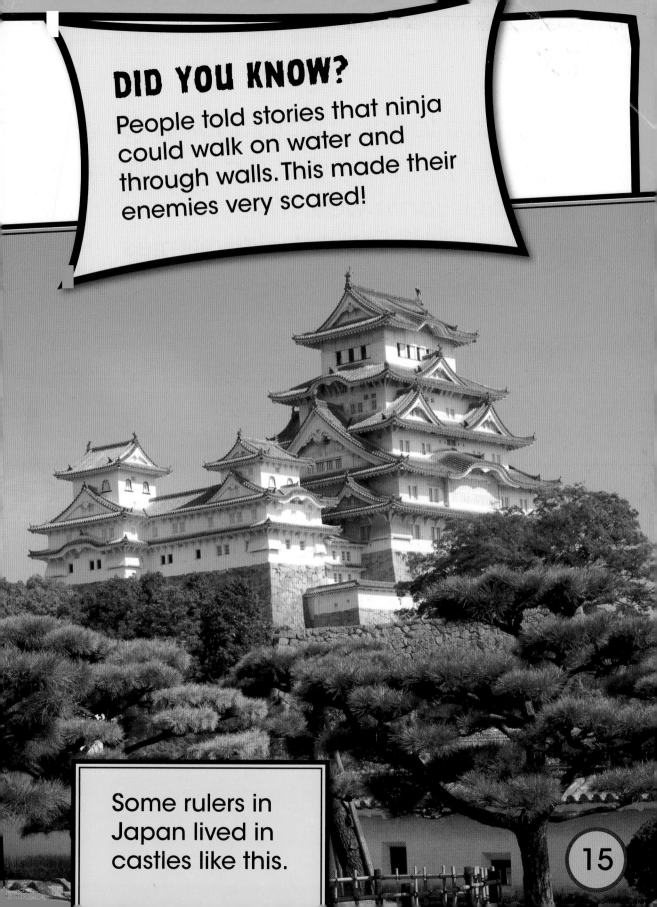

## DID YOU KNOW?

People told stories that ninja could walk on water and through walls. This made their enemies very scared!

Some rulers in Japan lived in castles like this.

Ninja had leaders called *jonin* (say *joe-neen*). Often ninja did not know who their *jonin* was. This meant the ninja could not tell their enemies where they lived.

Sometimes ninja disguised themselves as farmers.

Do you think this may be a secret ninja village?

## DID YOU KNOW?

Ninja lived in secret villages away from other people until it was time to go on a **mission**.

# Ninja weapons

A ninja's best weapon was his or her fists. They learned to fight quickly and trick their enemies. They also fought with chains, sticks, and swords.

Ninja also had special weapons that they could hide. They threw star-shaped knives at their **victims**. They even hid darts in their mouths that they could blow into their enemy's eyes.

*shuriken* - throwing star

Ninja were experts with many different weapons.

# Ninja skills

Ninja could hide in shadows and seem invisible. They used disguise so people couldn't recognise them. They walked in special ways so nobody could hear them coming.

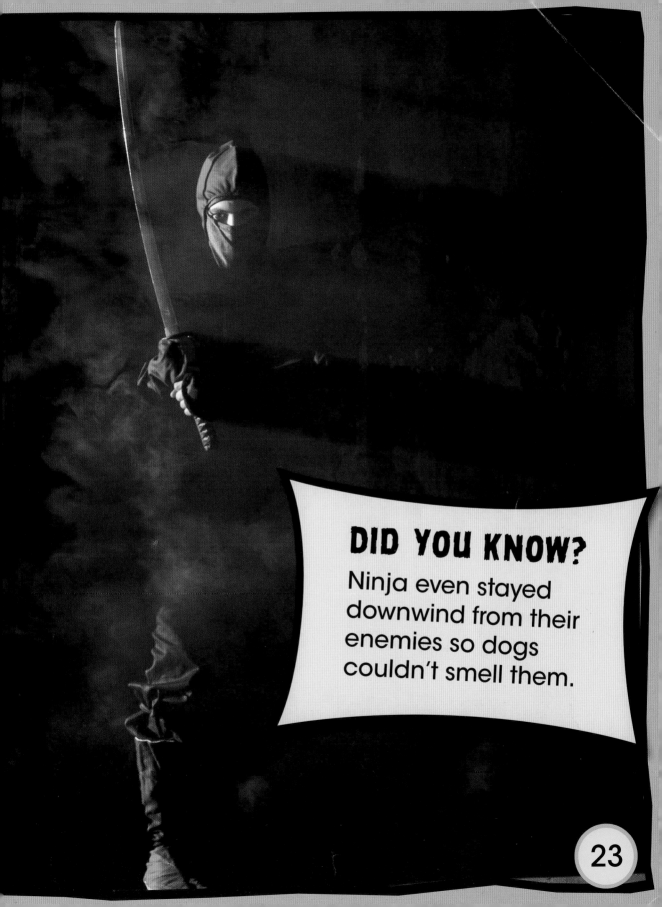

## DID YOU KNOW?

Ninja even stayed downwind from their enemies so dogs couldn't smell them.

Ninja used different skills when they were spying. They lived among their enemies and gathered information. They told their enemies lies to confuse them.

## DID YOU KNOW?

Ninja built secret escape tunnels in case they were found spying.

# The end of the ninja?

When the rulers in Japan stopped fighting there was no need for the ninja. Some ninja became **outlaws** and some became police. Ninja have become famous in stories, cartoons, and films.

The characters in Teenage Mutant Ninja Turtles use some of the skills that ninja used.

# Ninja activity

Can you move as silently as a ninja?
Try these ninja **stealth** moves:

## Move like a crane

Move slowly. Lift your knees high and
point your toes as you place your foot on
the ground. Ninja used this move to walk
through shallow water or dry leaves.

## Move like a crab

Bend your knees and move sideways quickly. Ninja used this move to sneak through shadows and passageways.

## Move like an octopus

Crouch down and slowly bring your back foot forward. Point the toes of this foot and feel the ground in front of you before putting it down. Then repeat with the new back foot. Sweep your hands in and out as you do this.

# Glossary

**assassin** person who murders others, often on orders

**defend** protect from danger or attack

**mission** special task, often secret

**outlaw** person who goes against the law

**stealth** secret or quiet

**victim** person who is attacked or hurt

# Find out more

## Books

*Combat Sports: Karate*, Clive Gifford
(Franklin Watts, 2008)

*Ninja*, Jason Glaser
(Capstone Edge Books, 2007)

*We're From Japan*, Victoria Parker
(Heinemann-Raintree, 2005)

## Places to visit

The British Museum, London
**www.britishmuseum.org/**

You can find out more about Japanese history in the
Japan Gallery at the British Museum.

**Find out**

Can you find out
about the clothes
ninja wore?

# Index